Tell Me WHY

ANIMAL
Questions and Answers

by
Rebecca Phillips-Bartlett

Minneapolis, Minnesota

Credits

All images are courtesy of Shutterstock.com, unless otherwise specified. With thanks to Getty Images, Thinkstock Photo, and iStockphoto.

Cover – BNP Design Studio, Guz Anna, Aliva, Anastacia Trapeznikova, Perfectorius, Qilli, Nattapol_Sritongcom, Ozlem Uluoca. Throughout – Guz Anna. 4 – GoodStudio, Harvepino. 6–7 – kwadrat70, Nadezda Barkova, StockSmartStart, Pravokrugulnik. 8–9 – Mr.Coffee, Petr, StockSmartStart. 10–11 – Lexi Claus, mamormoo, NadineVeresk, tonyzhao120. 12–13 – GlobalP, wannawit_vck. 14–15 – Maria.K-, Natalllenka.m, SLSK Photography. 17– Passakorn_14. 18– Dickov. 19 – jekjob, CoCoArt_Ua. 20 – alkir. 23– GlobalP.

Bearport Publishing Company Product Development Team

President: Jen Jenson; Director of Product Development: Spencer Brinker; Managing Editor: Allison Juda; Associate Editor: Naomi Reich; Associate Editor: Tiana Tran; Art Director: Colin O'Dea; Designer: Elena Klinkner; Designer: Kayla Eggert; Product Development Assistant: Owen Hamlin

Library of Congress Cataloging-in-Publication Data

Names: Phillips-Bartlett, Rebecca, 1999- author.
Title: Animal questions and answers / by Rebecca Phillips-Bartlett.
Description: Minneapolis, Minnesota : Bearport Publishing Company, [2024] | Series: Tell me why | Includes index.
Identifiers: LCCN 2023036844 (print) | LCCN 2023036845 (ebook) | ISBN 9798889163923 (library binding) | ISBN 9798889163978 (paperback) | ISBN 9798889164012 (ebook)
Subjects: LCSH: Animals--Miscellanea--Juvenile literature.
Classification: LCC QL49 .P45 2024 (print) | LCC QL49 (ebook) | DDC 590--dc23/eng/20230825
LC record available at https://lccn.loc.gov/2023036844
LC ebook record available at https://lccn.loc.gov/2023036845

© 2024 BookLife Publishing
This edition is published by arrangement with BookLife Publishing.

North American adaptations © 2024 Bearport Publishing Company. All rights reserved. No part of this publication may be reproduced in whole or in part, stored in any retrieval system, or transmitted in any form or by any means, electronic, mechanical, photocopying, recording, or otherwise, without written permission from the publisher.

For more information, write to Bearport Publishing, 5357 Penn Avenue South, Minneapolis, MN 55419.

Contents

Tell Me Why 4
Why Do Cats Land on Their Feet? 6
Why Do Zebras Have Stripes? 7
Why Do Animals Have Tails? 8
Why Do Giraffes Have Such Long Necks? 10
Why Are Owls Awake at Night? 11
Why Don't Penguins Fly? 12
Why Do Snakes Shed Their Skin? 13
Why Do Animals Hibernate? 14
Why Are Flamingos Pink? 16
Why Are Sloths So Slow? 17
Why Do Snails Need Slime? 18
Why Do Bats Hang Upside Down? 19
Why Do Animals Have Whiskers? 20
Asking Questions 22
Glossary 24
Index 24

TELL ME WHY

We share our planet with many different animals. Some live in the wild. Others join our families as pets in our homes.

QUESTION
What questions do you have about animals?

Animals are amazing, but they are all very different. They look different from one another and from us. Sometimes, the ways they act may seem strange! There are so many things about animals that leave us wondering **WHY?**

WHY DO CATS LAND ON THEIR FEET?

Cats have something called a righting **reflex**. This tells them which way is up. It helps cats turn their heads and bodies the right way so they almost always land on their feet.

Do not test this at home!

WHY DO ZEBRAS HAVE STRIPES?

A Zebra's stripes may help keep **insects** away! Scientists believe the stripes make it difficult for biting insects, such as horse flies, to tell how far away a zebra is. This makes it much harder for the bugs to land.

WHY DO ANIMALS HAVE TAILS?

There are many kinds of tails. And there are just as many reasons animals have them.

Squirrels use bushy tails to stay warm while they are sleeping. Their tails also help them balance while they are climbing.

Some monkeys need tails to help them balance and **navigate**. They use them to hold onto branches as they swing through the trees.

Dogs can **communicate** with their tails. A wag means these animals are happy.

WHY DO GIRAFFES HAVE SUCH LONG NECKS?

Scientists believe giraffes **evolved** to have longer necks to make mealtime easier. With more height, giraffes can reach higher up, where there are more leaves to eat.

WHY ARE OWLS AWAKE AT NIGHT?

Most owls are **nocturnal**, meaning they are awake at night. This helps the birds find plenty of food. Many of the small animals that owls eat are also awake at night.

FUN FACT

Not all owls are nocturnal. Look for the ones with brown or black eyes to spot who's awake at night.

WHY DON'T PENGUINS FLY?

Scientists believe birds can't be good at both flying and swimming. Penguins evolved to be in the water, making swimming important. These birds use their short, flipper-like wings to move through the water quickly. The wings that make penguins excellent swimmers are part of what makes it impossible for them to fly.

QUESTION
Would you rather be a wonderful swimmer or an amazing flyer?

FUN FACT
All animals shed their skin. But only some do it all at once.

WHY DO SNAKES SHED THEIR SKIN?

Snakes grow their whole lives, but their skin does not. Similar to when you grow out of your clothes, snakes grow out of their skin. When snakes get too big, a roomier layer of skin forms and they **shed** the old one.

HISSSS

WHY DO ANIMALS HIBERNATE?

Many animals **hibernate** to save their **energy** when the weather becomes too cold for them. Some animals, such as hedgehogs and some kinds of squirrels, hibernate through the winter because it's too cold for their bodies. There usually isn't enough food for them to eat either.

During the hot summer weather, some animals do something similar to hibernation called **estivation** (ES-tuh-*vay*-shuhn). These animals, such as desert tortoises, slow down and hide to stay cool in the hot, dry weather.

FUN FACT

Hibernation and estivation are not the same as sleeping. Many animals come out of these states just to get some sleep.

A desert tortoise

WHY ARE FLAMINGOS PINK?

You are what you eat! Or, at least flamingos are. These birds eat water plants and shrimp that are full of an orange and pink **pigment**. Over time, flamingos eat so much pigment that it turns their skin and feathers pink or orange.

FUN FACT
Baby flamingos are gray and turn pink during their first few years as they eat more and more.

WHY ARE SLOTHS SO SLOW?

Animals use energy when they move. Their bodies get energy from the food they eat. However, sloths take a really long time to turn their food into energy. These creatures need to move very slowly so they don't use up their energy too quickly.

WHY DO SNAILS NEED SLIME?

There are lots of reasons snails need slime. This sticky stuff helps snails stay on the surfaces they climb. It also helps them keep moisture around their bodies during dry weather.

WHY DO BATS HANG UPSIDE DOWN?

Bats hang upside down so they can take flight quickly. These winged creatures struggle to take off from the ground. To solve this problem, they climb up high and let themselves drop into the air. Hanging upside down is the perfect position for a quick getaway.

WHY DO ANIMALS HAVE WHISKERS?

Many animals have whiskers. They use them to tell how far away things are. Mice use whiskers to sense if they can fit through a gap.

When it's difficult to see with their eyes, animals depend on what they sense with their whiskers. Cats use them when they are hunting in the dark.

Seals use whiskers to sense movement from other animals when they're swimming through water.

Asking Questions

This book is full of questions you might have had about animals. How do we know the answers? Because many scientists have asked the same question!

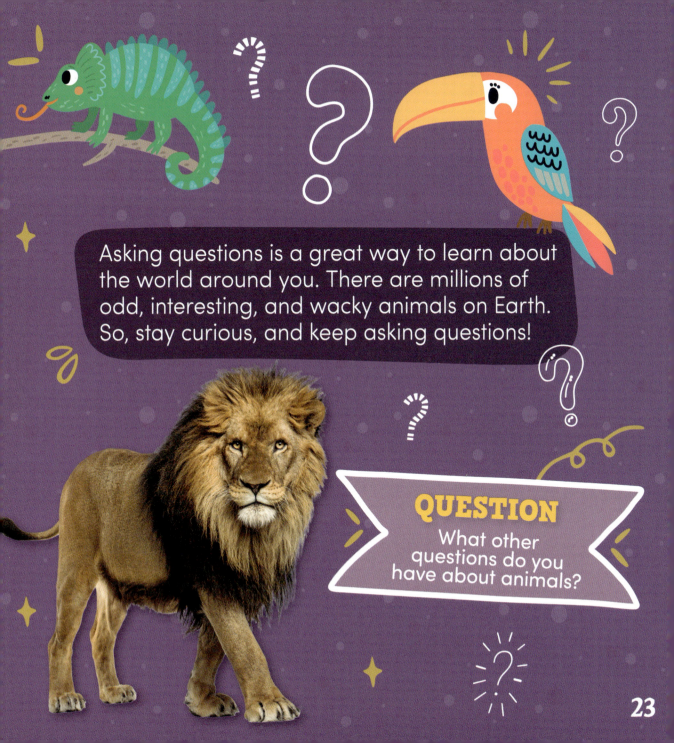

Asking questions is a great way to learn about the world around you. There are millions of odd, interesting, and wacky animals on Earth. So, stay curious, and keep asking questions!

QUESTION

What other questions do you have about animals?

Glossary

communicate to share information, needs, and feelings with others

energy the power needed by all living things to move, grow, and stay alive

estivation a sleeplike state that some animals enter to escape the heat

evolved changed slowly and naturally over time

hibernate to enter into a sleeplike state to wait out the cold

insects small animals that have six legs, three main body parts, and hard coverings

navigate to find one's way from place to place

nocturnal active mostly at night

pigment a substance that gives things color

reflex a movement or action that happens without someone trying

shed to lose a layer of skin

Index

energy 14, 17
flying 12, 19
leaves 10
night 11
reflex 6
skin 13, 16
sleep 8, 15
slime 18
stripes 7
summer 15
tails 8–9
whiskers 20–21
winter 14